GOD?

GOD?

NO There is NO GOD

JOE SULLIVAN/PAT BARRETT

Library of Congress Control Number:		2022904570
ISBN:	Hardcover	978-1-6698-1331-6
	Softcover	978-1-6698-1330-9
	eBook	978-1-6698-1329-3

Print information available on the last page.

Rev. date: 03/22/2022

To order additional copies of this book, contact:
Xlibris
844-714-8691
www.Xlibris.com
Orders@Xlibris.com
840130

Opening

"Look upon this book as being purely fictional, although it is based in part on the Bible, which I believe has its own stages of fiction"

I am a non practicing Catholic, and I believe in GOD; however, the purpose of this book is to question whether there really is a GOD.

During course of life, you have many questions; but no answers. However when you die and go to heaven, you hope to get those answers.

I, myself, have many; here are just a few:

1. Who really killed John F Kennedy?

2. What happened to Amelia Earhart?

3. How did Glen Miller disappear on his musical tour of World War II

4. What is really behind the Bermuda Triangle?

5. Are there really aliens out there?

But I realized that I would never get those answers because: There is no heaven; there are no answers.

The intention is to show the other side of the story, that there is No god; There are just too many questions without answers and too many answers that don't make sense.

I hope you enjoy the journey.

GOD bless you

The biggest question and the most troublesome that has bothered people of all religions is:

Why does GOD permit tragedies to occur, such as?"

"You lose a child"

"You are involved in a major accident"

"National disasters strike"

"Wars are happening all over the planet"

Have you ever given these tragedies any thought?"

The common answer to all of these is:

1. It's God's will

2. God works in mysterious ways

I can't buy these answers anymore!

It's a "cop out" because there is no intelligent answer.

God should not be responsible for the bad things that happen in life, and God should not be given the credit for the good things. There just isn't any God.

Many Christians give thanks to God for the good things in life, but do not blame God for the bad things. Well, God can't have it both ways. If God is to be given credit for the good things, then God must be blamed for the bad ones.

God can't have his cake and eat it too!

The Pope allegedly; represents God, although the Popes change, and they change how religion should be practiced. Does that mean that God changes his mind?

IE: No meat on Friday (this has changed); priests are not allowed to marry (change coming); women cannot become priests (change on the way)

Faith

The word "Faith" is used when" stupidity" is inappropriate. Catholic faith is built on a myth. I was raised a catholic; attended parochial schools and almost went into the seminary. I was always told that God can only do "good", God is good. As I got older, I saw too many tragic events take place for me NOT to question the existence of God. Faith is put to the test without question, believing God would allow all the pain and suffering and permit physical and moral evil as a mystery, and good will come as a result of that evil by ways we will know in eternal life.

Do you really believe this????

In every case, the appeal to faith is ultimately fallacious. By this definition, an appeal to faith is also an abandonment of reason; when one has no logical argument for a claim, they turn to faith as an explanation for their belief. Stating that you have faith in something might explain why you believe in it, but it does nothing to compel anyone else to believe the same way. The mere fact that one has faith in a belief system cannot possibly be considered reason enough for another to adopt that belief system as well.

Faith is often invoked in an argument when the person making a claim runs out of rational explanations to support his beliefs. It's a distraction from the fact that there is no real evidence.

Once faith enters the equation, the argument can quickly dissolve into absurdity, as absolutely any claim could be "supported" by faith.

For every story about how God, or religion, has brought about good things or events in a person's life, there are also religious people suffering. Believers experience hardship. They can get sick, suffer from depression, endure domestic abuse or die prematurely, just like anyone else. If God is really responsible for all these things that happen in a person's life, he must also be responsible for the bad things, or at least allow them to happen.

As mentioned, religion has also been responsible for a lot of terrible things throughout history, both on an institutional and personal level. If you accept that God is responsible for the good things that happen in a person's life, without evidence, how can you not also accept that God is responsible for people murdering their families, participating in religious wars or discriminating and harming others based on religious beliefs and viewpoints.

Just consider? Why does God allow a small, innocent child to fall through the ice and drown; was that God's will? A good God would not let that happen!

Why does a family of four die in a car crash? Was that also God's will?

Why are so many people murdered everyday throughout the world? Was this God's will again?

Why does more than 50% of the world population live in poverty? God's will?

These instances happen as a part of life, God has nothing to do with it.

"There is NO God"

Philippines

Many of the Filipinos are poor; many are starving and homeless. I have spent many years there, and have gotten to know the people and their lifestyles.

99% are Catholics, they believe in God. When I ask them why they accept poverty, and why they don't do something about changing their conditions, the answer I get is amazing: "This is what God has planned for us" A God would never plan, or wish for a people with meager means to live a life like that.

For your consideration:

Creation

God created both heaven and earth; but who made GOD???
Angels inhabit the heavens, and man the earth
Angels are spiritual creatures who glorify God and who work for the benefit of all.
Man was formed to rule the world over all creatures, and to serve God

Why then has God permitted "Bad" angels, Satan, etc., to exist?

God could have just eliminated these "Good" angels turned "Bad"

<u>Death</u>

Holy Father, why have thou forsaken me?

Jesus knew he was meant to die to save mankind; or did he?

<u>The Churches</u>

Why so many churches of different faiths???

("Matthew 2.16")

> "After Jesus was born, King Herod ordered children in Bethlehem who were two years old or under, to be killed, to wipe out a potential threat to HIM.
> How could God allow this?
> He couldn't: There is No God.

("4.17") Jesus says "Repent, for the kingdom of heaven is near! 2000+ years and counting....

("Matthew 4:20")

> "From that time Jesus began to preach, saying "Repent, for the kingdom of heaven is at hand"

"(Exodus 21:17")

> Whoever curses his father or his mother shall be put to death.

"(Exodus 33:80")

"And when Moses saw that the people had broken loose (for Aaron had let them break loose, to the derision of their enemies) then Moses stood in the gate of the camp and said," Who is on the Lord's side come with me" And all the sons of Levi gathered around him. And he said to them,'Thus, says the Lord God of Israel, put your sword by your side, each of you go to and from each gate throughout the camp, and each of you kill his brother and his companion and his neighbor. And the sons of the Lord did according to the word of Moses, and that day, 3,000 people were killed by their own people, per God's instructions.

Moses

40 years in the desert guiding the Jewish people to the promised land, and yet God would not permit him to enter, when they finally arrived.

Consider:
   Mary and Joseph had other children;
Consider:
   Jesus traveled no more than 30 miles from home and without the internet, he was a preacher and a prophet;
Consider:
   Why were the Jews God's chosen people; all God's children are supposed to be equal.

Consider:

God; Mohamed; Buddha, etc.

Consider:

Churches

Crimes of priests; corruption, the Vatican is the biggest bank in the world?

Consider:

God's angels, where did they come from??

Why did God select the Israelis as his "chosen people"?

Consider:

Deuteronomy

All of God's laws could never be obeyed

God was mad at Moses because Moses broke faith with him. God would not let

Moses enter the land of milk and honey, COME ON MAN, after all that Moses had been through, couldn't God show him a little mercy?

Genesis

God created earth (no other planet) so where did God come from?

Sodom and Gomorrah

Hundreds were killed by God, including innocent children

<u>Exodus</u>

Pharaoh of Egypt persecuted the Israelis, and it took God 10 plagues to force the Pharaoh to release the Jews to Moses.

Why did it take 10 plagues? God could have done it in 1! Also the 10th plague killed all the firstborn in Egypt.

<u>Aliens</u>

If God did send his only son to save mankind, then there can't be other "beings" living on other planets. If there are, then there is No God. If you believe in aliens, you can't believe in God. if you believe in God, you can't believe in aliens.

<u>Religion</u>

We do not need religion to be moral people. Only religious faith is strong enough to encourage misery, violence; terror; (abortion clinic bombings; terrorism; suicide bombers.) All commit their deadly acts based on their religious beliefs. These acts are committed in the name of religion. Religion is so wasteful; so extravagant.

Religion is a "placebo"

Religion is basically "guilt"

Religion is based on FEAR of future facts, and the leaders of the various religions keep the flames burning to keep their flock in line.

There is no life after death, and those who do believe it are only hoping there is. Religious doctrines are nothing but illusions.

Religion has ruled all people from Day1, and what has it done to the world? The world is falling apart; a degenerate society where violence, corruption, unhappiness seems to be the norm. Religion has lost many of its followers because people find it less credible.

Every religious story about how we got here is quite simply wrong. This is what all religions have in common

No 6 day work, 1 day rest, no Valhalla, no Olympus.

Documents are not self- authenticating

Just because something is written in a book does not mean it's true. This is obvious. There are millions of fictional stories throughout history and plenty of other books that claim to be factual, but have been proven to be false. The existence of scripture does not automatically prove anything about the veracity of what those scriptures contain.

Christianity vs Islam

Christian bible states that to enter heaven, you must believe in Jesus as your savior.

Islam Quran states that non Muslims will end up in hell; so if you believe in "God" you must pick the right religion. However not every region supports heaven or hell. Falling back on faith is used when one has no rational justification for explanations. Every holy book is full of inconsistent and inaccurate errors (Bible and Quran)

Religion does give consolation and comfort, and is a tool used by the ruling class to subjugate the underclass.

A miracle goes against the laws of nature and must be proved by evidence if it is to be believed; and this has never happened.

People are "good" (have morals) without any connection to God. If God wanted to forgive the sins of mankind, why not just forgive them, instead of having his only son tortured and murdered.

Are you aware religion is behind every war?

Are things moral simply because God says so? Or does God give certain orders because they are inherently moral? This is the question at the core of Plato's Euthyphro dilemma, a problem that lies at the heart of religious debates about the divinity of moral authority. If morality exists separate from God's will, there is no reason to rely on God for moral behavior; one could have moral standards independently without divine feedback.

On the other hand, if God creates morality simply by saying whether something is right or wrong, then that's not really morality; it's arbitrariness. Morality would become nothing more than the whimsy of a divine being blindly followed by humans.

Most religions claim an all-powerful, all loving benevolent deity. However, physical reality often contradicts this claim. Terrible things happen to people every day. Children die tragically young; natural disasters wipe out whole communities and people die from accidents and disease. These do not suggest a righteous and compassionate God. These suggest that God is either powerless, cruel, or non-existent. If the Christian religion is the "right" one, every Muslim, Hindu, Buddhist and Jew would burn in hell for eternity (John 3:18-36, 2 Thessalonians 1:6-10 and Revelation 21:8), and this rule is the same for other religions that believe in the concept of hell, such a Islam:

And whoever desires other than Islam as religion-never will it be accepted from him, and he, in the Hereafter, will be among the losers, (Quran 3.85)

In the garden of Eden, Adam disobeyed God by eating the forbidden fruit...he had sinned.

Because of this ALL men were considered to be sinners. The whole human race is affected by Adam's sin. REALLY? God gave woman menopause because of Eve's misbehavior in the Garden of Eden. But it was Adam that ate the damn apple, why didn't he get menopause also?

("Romans 6.6")

Therefore, just as sin came into the world through one man, and death through sin, and so death spread to all men because all sinned.

Bible also allows slavery:

("Timothy 1.6")

"Let all who are under a yoke as bond-servants regard their own masters as worthy of all honor, so that the name of God and and the teaching may not be reviled. Those who have believing masters must not be disrespectful on the ground that they are brothers; rather they must serve all the better since those who benefit by their good service are believers and beloved.

Indeed, religions do seem to incite violence. This does not always imply a direct causal relationship between religion and violence, yet, this is the opposite of what you'd expect if morality really did stem from God.

Consider, for example, the issue of slavery. Although there are some people who still believe that slavery is moral, the vast majority of modern Christians are unlikely to admit support for the ownership of another person. Nevertheless, the Bible has many references to slavery, carefully detailing the rules for proper slave ownership.

Slavery isn't the only questionable practice mentioned in the Bible. The death penalty was also wielded quite liberally in biblical times, and death was a popular punishment for sins in the Old Testament, including violations such as adultery (Leviticus 20:13), homosexuality (Leviticus 20:13), lying about virginity (Deuteronomy 22:13-21), breaking the Sabbath (Exodus 31:14), cursing your parents (Exodus 21:17) and more.

In Islamic teaching, it's made quite clear that anyone who turns away from Islam should be put to death. Within some of the most trusted and authoritative Hadih collections in Islam, which is the main source of Islamic laws and ethics Prophet Muhammad is quoted as calling for the death penalty against apostates.

Kindness for Poor Brothers

If your brother becomes poor and cannot maintain himself with you, you shall support him as though he were a stranger and a sojourner, and he shall live with you. Take no interest from him or profit, but fear your God, that your brother may live beside you. You shall not lend him your money at interest, nor give him your food for profit. I am the Lord your God, who brought you out of the land of Egypt to give you the land of Canaan, and to be your God.

If your brother becomes poor beside you and sells himself to you, you shall not make him a slave as a slave: he shall be with you as a hired worker as a sojourner.

He shall serve with you until the year of the jubilee. Then he shall go out from you, he and his children with him, and go back to his own clan and return to the possession of his fathers. For they are my servants, whom I brought out of the land of Egypt; they shall not be sold as slaves. You shall not rule over him ruthlessly but shall fear your God As for your male and female slaves whom you may have: you may buy male and female slaves from among the nations that are around you. You may also buy from among the strangers who sojourn with you and their clans that are with you, who have been born in your land, and they may be your property.

You may bequeath them to your sons after you to inherit as a possession forever. You may make slaves of them, but over your brothers the people of Israel you shall not rule, one over another ruthlessly.

Bible also allows Rape: Female captives can be raped:

(Numbers 32:40, 31:18)

"But all the young girls who have not known man by lying with him keep alive for yourselves"

(Zechariah 12:14)

"The Coming day of the Lord"

Behold, a day is coming for the Lord when,: the spoil taken from you will be divide in your midst. For I will gather all nations against Jerusalem to battle and the city shall be taken and the houses plundered and the women raped."

Disobedient children can be beaten with rods

A Rebellious Son

(Deuteronomy 11:11)

"if a man has a stubborn and rebellious son who will not obey the voice of his father or the voice of his mother, and, though they discipline him, will not listen to them, then the father and his mother shall take hold of him and bring him out to the elders of his city at the gate of the place where he lives, and they shall say to the elders of his city, "This our son is stubborn and rebellious; he will not obey our voice; he is a glutton and a drunkard" Then all the men of the city shall stone him to death with stones. So you shall purge the evil from your midst, and all Israel shall hear and fear"

Children may be sacrificed to God in return for any aid in battle.

Even Jesus said"

1. Family members should hate one another so that they could love Jesus more.

2. Promises salvation to those who abandon their wives and children for him.

3. The rod is not enough for children who curse their parents; they must be killed.

So much for God's and Jesus's moral values

Bible IS morally inconsistent. The Bible and the Quran were written by many authors and interpreted by many writers, so many discrepancies are seen throughout.

God is omnipresent; all knowing; all merciful, yet at times he behaves like a tyrant.

Are you aware many people discussed in the scriptures are only "legends" with no proof they ever existed. Many stories; like "Noah's Ark" are absurdities. These stories are fictitious, not history.

The origin of the universe is unknown; we just don't know! Not knowing however, does not give us the right to make something up, (like God created the universe).

Burden of Proof

Where is there any evidence that God exists?????

Believing in God is the same as saying "I don't know", when it comes to trying to explain things that can't be understood.

If God created all things, then who created God?

How could God permit so much suffering in this world?

How could God permit hundreds of Christian denominations, all which believe that others are wrong.

Missionaries convinced people the world over that their gods were false, and the Missionaries were the only true God; we taught them to "switch" to our God.

How could God permit so much suffering in this world?

Religious texts are man-made and fallible

There's a simple explanation for the errors in the Quran and Bible: these documents were written by humans, and in many cases, were stitched together from oral traditions and transcribed decades or even centuries after the events described. Bear in mind, also, that the books of the Bible are largely anonymous. Names like Matthew, Luke, and John were added after the fact by editors and scribes. The actual identity of these authors is unknown.

Biblical scholars estimate that the oldest books of the New Testament, Paul's letters, were written around 20 years after the date of Christ's supposed resurrection. Paul was not present for any of the events described in the gospels, and he did not know Jesus personally. The gospels themselves were written even later, between 30 and 70 years after the alleged death of Jesus.

- So many paradoxes in the bible:

An eye for an eye vs turn the the check love thy neighbor and hate thy enemy vs love thy enemy: bless them Religious beliefs are irrational; sometimes it drives sensible people to commit violent acts. Morals are credited to God; if there is NO God, then people wouldn't have any morals; God dictates morals to man. If this is so, then how does one account for God's actions in:

1. Punishing people for sins of others

2. Punishes all mothers with painful childbirth

3. Kills all first born sons

There are many more samples detailed in the Bible.

No, God did not have anything to do with the morals of mankind

There is no proof, evidence of a "deity"; wanting to believe something doesn't make it true.

The holy scriptures (Scrolls) contain so much contradictory information; it compares to the survey that CPA firms make when asking different IRS offices the same question; they get all different answers.

The question of prayer is self contradictory

When considering the supposed power of prayer, it's important to look at the big picture. Every day, people die, divorce, become disabled, lose their jobs, or live in poverty. It's reasonable to assume that many of these people are praying for better circumstances without receiving any divine assistance. Similarly, consider that many prayers are inherently selfish. While you pray for your niece to get a much needed heart transplant, someone else is praying for his organ donor's son's life to be spared. Whether you're praying to win a war or a football game, you're also praying for the people on opposing side to lose. To assume that God is not only personally invested in the minutiae of your life but your problems are ultimately more important than other problems he may be asked to solve is both selfish and absurd considering the incredible amount of individual problems and concerns of every human on this planet.

Within religious circles, this issue becomes more insidious. Working from the assumption that God is good, hears all prayers, many believers of God offer a few possible explanations for why a prayer is not answered:

You prayed incorrectly

You don't believe hard enough

God doesn't see fit to grant your wish

People suffer even without prayer. Peoples prayers when not granted leave those people depressed. Prayers are meaningless, so maybe doing something more constructive would be more helpful like; offering moral support, volunteering, to name a couple ideas.

Jesus demanded "Faith" throughout the Bible and he never recommended "Knowledge."

Very important. The Tree of Knowledge in the Garden of Eden. God forbid Adam and Eve from eating the fruit from the "Tree of Knowledge". Why? God did not want man having knowledge of any kind; he wanted man to have "faith" only. No knowledge; no questions; just blind faith.

Many respected people throughout the world do not believe in God (Albert Einstein), actually most scientists.

Science is the enemy of religion; religious beliefs cannot be proven, and fall under the category of "intellectual rubbish"

No One Knows That Day and How

"But concerning that day and hour no one knows, not even the angels of heaven, nor the Son, but the Father only."

Matthew, Luke and Mark all "quoted" Jesus as saying that he would come back in their lifetimes. This did not happen.

Various religions all have interpretations of Jesus's remarks, but none have come to pass.

Why God was so clear in the Bible, yet so obscure in the world?

Jesus and the apostles were accused of practicing magic, and indeed they did. Sometimes these magic tricks were described as "miracles". Did you know gospels are nothing but ancient fiction?

Believe in God, even if you don't, because if you are wrong, you face eternal damnation.

Gentiles invented many gods. Believing there is no God means that the suffering we incur in life isn't caused by some omniscient force that can't be bothered to help us. One can help himself or theirs without relying on a deity that doesn't exist.

You have all these "prophets" predicting the exact day of the end of the word.

When that doesn't happen, they change the date.(all based on the bible).

People have a need for this type of news; they have to know when the end of the world would end so they can prepare.

Many, many prophesies re "end of the world" all interpreted somewhere in the bible; all failed.

God made Adam and Eve..and nobody else??

How did people of color come to be? Ie: Blacks, Brown, Red, Yellow etc. How did physical changes develop, Asians, Indians, etc.

The devil, who was he?

How did he come to be?

Is there such a being?

Sermon on the Mount:

Whoever marries a divorced woman commits adultery "Matthew(5.33)"

Divorce-

It was also said, "Whoever divorces his wife, let him give her a certificate of divorce. But I say to you that everyone who divorces his wife, except on the ground of sexual immorality, makes her commit adultery, and whoever marries a divorced woman commits adultery.

When Jesus was preaching in the synagogue, his mother, Mary, along with her other children, went to see him.

(Matthew 13.15) Jesus' Mother and Brothers)

While he was still speaking to the people, behold, his mother and brothers stood outside, asking to speak to him. But he replied to the man who told him, "Who is my mother, and who are my brothers?". And stretching out his hand toward his disciples, he said, "Here are my mother and my brothers! For whoever does the will of my Father in heaven is my brother and sister and mother". He didn't have time for his mother. One of God's commandments is to honor thy mother and thy father. Jesus says that he is the son of God?, but breaks God's own commandment.

Not peace but a sword

"(Matthew 10.5)" Not Peace but a Sword

"Do not think I have come to bring peace to the earth. I have not come to bring peace but a sword. For I have come to set a man against his father, and a daughter against her mother, and a daughter-in-law against her mother-in law. And a person's enemies will be those of his own household. Whoever loves father or mother more than me is not worthy of me, and whoever loves son or daughter more than me is not worthy of me."

("Matthew 13.15") The Purpose of the Parables)

Then the disciples came and said to him, "Why do you speak to people in parables?", And he answered them, "To you it has been given to know the secrets of the kingdom of heaven, but to them it has not been given. For to the one who has, more will be given, and he will have an abundance, but from the one who has not, even what he has will be taken away. This is why I speak to them in parables, because seeing they do not see, and hearing they do not hear, nor do they understand. Indeed, in their case the prophecy of Isaiah is fulfilled that says:

"You will indeed hear but never understand,

and you will indeed see but never perceive,

For this people's heart has grown dull, and with their ears they can barely hear, and their eyes have closed, lest they should see with their eyes and hear with their ears and understand with their heart and turn, and I would heal them."

But blessed are your eyes, for they see, and your ears, for they hear. For truly, I say to you, many prophets and righteous people longed to see, and did not see it, and to hear what you hear, and did not hear it. He said that they would not truly understand otherwise; but it only confused the people, not help them to understand what he was trying to say.

This seems to only be the way of "coping out"

(Deuteronomy 6:1-2) A Chosen People

"When the Lord your God brings you into the land that you ate entering to take possession of it, and clears away many nations before you the Hittites, the Girgashites, the Amorites, the Canaanites, the Perizzites, the Hivites, and the Jebusites, seven nations more numerous and mightier than you, and when the Lord your God gives them over to you and you defeat them, then you must devote them to complete destruction. You shall make no covenant with them and show no mercy to them. You shall not intermarry with them, giving your daughters to their sons or taking their daughters for your sons, for they would turn away your sons from following me, to serve other gods. Then the anger of the LORD would be kindled against you, and hewould destroy you quickly. But thus shall you deal with them: you shall break down their altars and dash in pieces their pillars and chop down their Asherim and burn their carved images with fire.

"The Great Day of the Lord is Coming"

From Malachi to gospel of Matthew; 400 years of silence...400 years with no word from God; no miracles; nothing...

Matthew

Jesus was led by the spirit into the wilderness to be tempted by the devil. After fasting forty days and nights, Jesus was hungry. The devil said to Jesus; command these stones to become loaves of bread; Jesus rebuked him. Then the devil took Jesus high in a pinnacle of the temple, and said to Jesus throw yourself down; again Jesus rebuked him. Then the devil took Jesus to a very high mountain, and showed him all of the kingdoms of the world, and their glory. All these things I will give to you if you fall down and worship me. Jesus again rebuked him. How did Matthew know all these things?; Jesus was alone: there was no one with him.

("Malachi 4.6") The Great Day of the Lord

"For behold, the day is coming, burning like an oven, when all the arrogant and all evildoers will be stubble. The day that is coming shall set them ablaze, says the Lord of hosts, so that it will leave them neither root nor branch. But for you who fear my name, the sun of righteousness shall rise with healing in its wings. You shall go out leaping like calves from the stall. And you shall tread down the wicked, and for they will be ashes under the soles of your feet, on the day when I act, says the Lord of hosts.

"Remember the law of my servant Moses, the statutes and rules that I commanded him at Horeb for all Israel.

"Behold, I will send you Elijah the prophet before the great and awesome day of the Lord comes. And he will turn the hearts of fathers to their children and the hearts of children to their fathers, lest I come and strike the land with a decree of utter destruction"

Why has God stood by the Israelis, called them his chosen people, when they disobeyed him so many times? God would not permit Israelis to marry into other tribes.

Year 2021, still waiting for the "second coming". While waiting for all to rise, these souls are in purgatory? When someone you love dies, you tell young ones, that they went to heaven. That is not true, because God has presumably not judged them yet.

It is safer to believe in God than be wrong and go to Hell. In the mid-1600s, mathematician and philosopher Blaise Pascal introduced an argument that could be called Pascal's Wager. His argument discuses the issues of religious belief from a mathematical standpoint, determining that the cost of belief is lower than the cost of atheism.

The wage takes the following format:

If you believe in God, and he does exist, you will be rewarded with eternity in Heaven.

If you believe in God and he does not exist, nothing will happen to you.

If you reject belief in God and he does exist, you will be doomed to an eternity in Hell.

If you don't believe in God, and he doesn't exist, nothing will happen to you. Based on these suppositions, Pascal reasons that it is always safer to live as though God is real because if there is a God and you believe in him, the benefits are infinite. If you believe in God and turn out to be wrong, you will have lost nothing; if you don't believe in God and turn out to be wrong, the consequences are dire.

Pascal was an admittedly brilliant mathematician, and his contributions to mathematics are valuable. As a theological argument, however, Pascal's Wager breaks down for several important reasons. First, it's important to realize the wager does nothing to prove the nature of God. It's not an argument for the existence of god at all, actually; it's an argument against atheism based on the relative opportunity vs cost of belief.

Second, you must recognize the limitations of Pascal's premise, as a Christian apologist, his argument works only for the Christian God. It ignores the the possibility of any other deity and assumes that the motives of God are consistent with the teachings of basic Christian theology. Viewed in the context of world religions, the wager falls apart completely. The wager is based on the mathematics analysis of four outcomes. However, if you throw the multitude of world religions into the equation, the premises and mathematician analysis becomes much more complex and convoluted, making your chances of successful wager significantly slimmer.

When baseball players get a hit, they bless themselves and point up to heaven, thanking God for the hit.

But, should they strike out, there is no blaming God. God has nothing to do with a player having a good game, or a bad one. There is No God.

When you go to church to light a candle and pray for a certain thing, if you get it, you thank God and the cost of that candle was a good investment. But what if you don't get it, can you get a refund?

What if the world discovered or found out there is no God??

Did you ever ask yourself?

What was God doing before he created the world??????

Noah's Ark

Destruction of Babylon; God couldn't find good people? The good people were hiding.

Jericho, are you kidding me? No "miracles" in hundreds of years; where are the current good deeds?

A being who allows so much suffering; No. No.

Don't get me wrong, I believe in God, but there is a little voice in me that keeps on saying: There is NO God

As co author, I wanted to share some thoughts of mine:

I too, was raised in a very Catholic home, both parents were devote Catholics. As a young teen I was asked by our local Priest if I would teach Sunday school to 5th grade boys, of course I agreed. Little did I realize, how much my eyes were to open very wide in a questioning way.

By now I was around age 14-15 when I began to ask "why is it NOT alright to eat meat on Friday? Then the church changed to telling us we could eat meat; also why were women required to wear something on their heads when attending mass; then the church requirement changed to allow women to wear hats; it was a very confusing time.

One very disturbing message from the Pope had to do with Saint Paul, Patron saint for safety and protection. The Pope announced St. Paul was no longer a Saint! Gosh we all had St Paul's metals on our car visors; we believed in him! Did this mean I had to "stop believing" in St. Paul? Or God? or the Pope? No one could answer me; I felt very alone and the loneliness paved the way for me to leave the catholic church.

As the years past, I found my own path to "talking" out loud; usually near a body of water; it was always and still is very refreshing and lends itself to getting the answers I seek.

Thank you for listening and wishing you all the best!

Epilogue

I hope you found this book somewhat interesting, and if you still believe in a God, then you might want to look into:

The Easter Bunny

The Tooth Fairy, and yes, don't forget,

Santa Claus

.